My Favorite Machines

Cars

Colleen Ruck

Smart Apple Media

Smart Apple Media
P.O. Box 3263, Mankato, MN 56002

 An Appleseed Editions book

Planning and production by Discovery Books Limited
Designed by D.R ink
Edited by Colleen Ruck

Library of Congress Cataloging-in-Publication Data

Ruck, Colleen.
  Cars / by Colleen Ruck.
      p. cm. -- (My favorite machines)
  Includes index.
  ISBN 978-1-59920-673-8 (library binding)
  1. Automobiles--Juvenile literature. I. Title.
  TL147.R825 2012
  629.222--dc22
                            2011010310

Photograph acknowledgments
Getty Images: pp. 10 (Hulton Archive), 19 (Jeff J. Mitchell); Istockphoto.com: pp. 5, 17 (Chris Seely); Pagani Communication: p. 9; Porsche: p. 7; Rex Features: p. 21 (Jim Smeal/BEI); Shelby Supercars: p. 8; Shutterstock: pp. 4 (Max Earey), 5 bottom (Siamionau Pavel), 6 (Digitalsportphotoagency), 11 (Lukasz Bizon), 12 (Nikos Douzinas), 13 (Elemer Sagi), 14 (manzrussali), 15 (Max Earey), 16 (Sternstuden), 18 (galimaufry), 20 (Olga Besnard), 22 (Peter Weber), 23 (Tatiana Belova), Wikimedia: p. 19 (Erik Christensen).

Cover photo: Shutterstock (Oksana.perkins)

Printed in the United States of America at Corporate Graphics
In North Mankato, Minnesota

DAD0502
52011

9 8 7 6 5 4 3 2 1

Contents

Cars Everywhere

People use cars to travel from one place to another.

A car is powered by an **engine**. The driver uses the steering wheel to turn the car's wheels.

Sports Cars

Sports cars like this Ford GT are speedy and fun to drive.

This Porsche has a roof that folds away.

Supercars

Supercars are the fastest and most powerful cars on the road. This is an SSC Ultimate Aero.

Exhaust pipes

The fumes made by the engine leave the car through its **exhaust pipe.** This Pagani Zonda has four exhaust pipes.

Early Cars

Starting handle

The first cars had a soft, fold-down roof. Drivers started their cars by turning a wind-up handle.

1911
Model T Ford Torpedo Roadster
Owners: John and Marry Ellen Barr

Today, some people collect old cars and take them to shows and fairs.

Rally Cars

Rally cars race on roads,
gravel tracks, and dirt tracks.
They even race over snow and ice.

12

Sometimes, rally cars look like they are flying over the bumpy ground.

Race Cars

Race cars are fast and noisy.
They have powerful engines.

Some race cars reach speeds
of 220 miles (355 kilometers)
per hour.

15

Off the Road

Some cars can be used for off-road driving. Farmers drive them, but they can be used just for fun, too.

The huge **tires** on this off-road car help it grip the ground. They make traveling over rough ground easier.

In the City

Small cars are good for city driving. They are cheap to run and easy to park, like this Smart car.

This is an electric car. Its engine is powered by a **battery** instead of **gasoline**.

Cars for Luxury

Luxury cars are larger than normal family cars. This luxury car has a TV and a **refrigerator** in the back!

Celebrities such as film stars use luxury cars to travel to special **events**.

Custom Cars

People sometimes paint their cars to make them stand out. Look at the bright, colorful paint job on this car!

Stretch limos are huge custom cars. People can hire them for weddings and special outings.

Glossary

battery	An object that stores electric power, for example in a flashlight or a car.
celebrity	A famous person.
engine	The part of a car where the power comes from to make it move.
event	An organized activity.
exhaust pipe	A pipe that carries gases from a car engine.
fumes	Smelly gases and smoke that can be poisonous.
gasoline	Fuel used in cars and trucks.
gravel	Small stones used for making roads or paths.
refrigerator	We keep food and drinks cold and fresh in a metal cupboard called a refrigerator.
tire	A thick piece of rubber that goes around a wheel.

Web sites

www.shelbysupercars.com
Home of the world's fastest supercar.

http://sv.berkeley.edu/showcase/flash/car.html
Design a car and test it on a race track

http://auto.howstuffworks.com/car.htm
Learn about how different parts of a car work.

Index

24